Just Mini Desserts

Quick and Easy Mini Desserts
for Casual Entertaining

by Robert Zollweg

Written and Designed by Robert Zollweg
Photography by Rick Luettke, Luettke Studio.com
Graphics by Gary Raschke and Sandy Shultz
Art Direction by Gary Raschke

Library of Congress Cataloging-in-Publication Data:

Just Mini Desserts, Quick and Easy Mini Desserts
Recipes for Casual Entertaining / Robert Zollweg

ISBN 978-0-578-05816-0

Printed in the United States
by RR Donnelley and Company

This book is dedicated in loving memory to my friend and colleague,
Gretchen Gotthart Skeldon

and to my two very special children,
Christopher and Rhonda
and their mother, Elaine.

To my mother, Virginia and to my wonderful and understanding family.

A special dedication to Steven,
my partner, who has stood by me for over thirty years.

A very special thanks to Gary Raschke, without his help and guidance,
his graphic knowledge, his art direction, his patience, this book probably
would never have happened.

To Bill Muzzillo, my friend at the beach who saw my vision and
encouraged me to go for it.

And Sandy Shultz, my friend and associate, a superb graphic designer, who always
goes above and beyond what is expected of her every day.

To Libbey Glass, a company I have worked for for over forty years and
can say that I have loved every minute of it.
A great company, with great people that produces great product.
You could not ask for anything more.

Contents

Introduction

Just Mini Desserts is all about serving several delicious desserts in little mini servings, it's that simple. But beyond that, it's about presentation. Utilizing various sizes of containers and dishes that creates something your guests will enjoy. You probably wouldn't bother making mini desserts just for 2 or 3 people, but you would when it's about entertaining, having friends and family over and being a great host or hostess. Making your guests feel welcome and at home, that's what entertaining is all about and Just Mini Desserts is here to help you create that experience.

I first heard about the whole mini dessert trend at the National Restaurant Show in Chicago. At the time, restaurants were seeing a decline in larger, over the top desserts and recognized that many of the guests were watching their weight or being more calorie conscious. As a result, they started developing and serving petite versions or mini-desserts. To make them special and more exciting, they found small glass and ceramic containers to show off their new creations. As a result, mini desserts have taken the foodservice industry by storm. They are usually served in multiples with a variety of different mini-desserts to choose from. I felt this was something today's consumers would love to try at home and were missing in the marketplace, especially when it came to home entertaining. Most of the following mini desserts are pretty quick and simple to make. This is important with today's lifestyles in home entertaining. Nobody has the time nor patience to spend hours in the kitchen preparing and cleaning up from a complicated recipe. This is a little unfortunate, but true.

Mini desserts are usually served in various 2 to 3 ounce containers or dessert dishes with a number of different desserts. This is so all your guests can try a small sampling of a few desserts without feeling terribly guilty or just because they want to try them all.

Displaying mini desserts is also a key component in entertaining. Presenting them on a variety of different serving and tiered trays helps with this fashionable and trendy presentation. See photos on the following pages for a few creative ideas. These presentations are great for special parties, wedding showers and birthdays, to name a few. You will look very professional and your guests will love you and look forward to another one of your parties or get togethers.

I hope you enjoy these wonderful little mini desserts as much as I have in creating them. They are quick, simple and fun to make.

I'd like to thank Libbey Glass for giving me the opportunity to fulfill my dream of working in the tabletop industry for all these years and where I have learned so much about entertaining. I love to entertain and mini desserts are a great way to turn a special occasion into something really special.

Enjoy !   Robert Zollweg

Serving Suggestions, Containers and Preparation

When do you serve mini desserts? I serve them whenever I'm having a get together, usually when I'm entertaining at least 8 or more people. That way I can make several different recipes that everyone will enjoy.

For a fabulous dessert table you can use your kitchen counter, a small card table set up in the living room or family room, wherever you decide to serve. The extra effort with your presentation makes all the difference in the world.

Use a couple of glass-tiered serving pieces, some white ceramic rectangular serving trays and, of course, a variety of different mini-desserts. Compliment these mini desserts with special coffees, teas, dessert wines, cognacs or flavored liqueurs served in small cordial glasses. Remember, it's all about presentation and making your guests feel special and at home.

Serving Presentations

Here, I'm showing a simple dessert setting using a variety of different mini desserts on some square and rectangular platters and servers. They can be made of glass, ceramic or stainless steel. Use flavored teas and dessert coffees to compliment your mini desserts. This is a wonderful presentation when served a little later on in the evening after dinner or after you have finished playing cards or a favorite family game.

This is a chocolate lover's dream: a chocolate mini dessert buffet. Using a variety of chocolate mini desserts, serve your guests complimenting wines and fancy liqueurs in beautiful cordial glasses. Go to your local grocery store wine department and ask the wine specialist about what is a good wine or brandy to serve with chocolate. This will take very little effort and you will love it. I love to serve my chocolate mini dessert buffet when all my friends come back to my house after our neighborhood holiday house tours. It's light and delicious and warms them up inside and out.

Containers

There are so many wonderful containers in the marketplace that can be used to serve mini desserts. Use your imagination. Glass makes a wonderful medium because you can see the layering of the ingredients with all the colors and textures. Small ceramic ramekins work best for baking.

Many of your favorite desserts can be made into mini desserts. If you cannot prepare them in small dishes, you can always serve them in small dishes.

Be creative, there are many choices of mini dessert containers to choose from. The containers I used in this publication can be purchased from various retailers or you can go to www.libbey.com and order them on line.

These packaged gift sets of Just Desserts are available at most area retailers or you can purchase them on line at www.libbey.com/just desserts

Preparation

There are a number of different tools in the marketplace that make it easier to fill these small dessert dishes. Pictured above is a commercial decorating press and filling tool, but you can use a simple pastry bag or even a one quart storage bag with the corner cut off. Both can be purchased at your area retailers. They are very helpful in filling the smaller items and can also add fancy swirls "to give your creations that professonal touch". I love to use them. They are simple to operate and very easy to clean.

I like using a standard kitchen funnel for filling the small mini containers that have small openings. The one at the right has a stopper type plunger to turn the flow on and off. I like using them for practically everything. They are inexpensive and pretty easy to clean. They help with the filling and in keeping the dessert away from the sides of the container for a cleaner presentation.

Simple Parfaits

Strawberry Budini Parfaits

I love to use tall cordial glasses when serving this dessert, they make such a spectacular presentation. You'll need 12 of them, about 3-4 oz each. See photo at right.

1 - 8 oz pkg cream cheese
6 tbsp sweet marsala cheese, divided in half
4 tbsp whipping cream or heavy cream
3 tbsp sugar
2 cups sliced strawberries or raspberries or blueberries
2 cups coarsely crumbled macaroon or sugar cookies

Combine cream cheese, 3 tbsp marsala cheese, whipping cream & 2 tbsp sugar in a mixing bowl, stir until blended. Set aside.

Combine strawberries, 3 tbsps marsala, 1 tbsp sugar in a mixing bowl. Toss to blend. Refrigerate for 30 minutes.

Place a heaping spoonful of cookie crumbs in the bottom of the cordial glasses. Fill the cordials with the strawberry mixture to just about full. Top berries with the cream cheese mixture and sprinkle with cookie crumbs or a fresh strawberry.

Chill 30 minutes. Serve and Enjoy !

Cherry Macaroon Parfaits

This dessert is quick, easy and just as delicious. Almost any small 3 oz glass container will work. I love using the mini parfaits. You will need 12 of them. See photo at right.

1 small box of vanilla pudding, cooked type is a little creamier
2 cups cold milk
1 small can cherry pie filling, 20 oz.
     (blueberry or strawberry pie filling works as well)
1/4 tsp almond extract
6 macaroon or sugar cookies, coarsely crumbled

Almost any shortbread cookie will work here, but the macaroons add a unique twist to the combined flavors.

Make the pudding as directed on the box. Combine the cherry pie filling and the almond extract. You can layer this dessert or just start with a layer of pudding, then some cookie crumbs, a spoonful of cherries and top it off with some cookie crumbs. Refrigerate and Serve.   Enjoy !

Strawberry Cream Parfaits

This is one of those simple little desserts that is especially delicious when made at the height of strawberry season, when the berries are real sweet and juicy. You will need 12 dessert glasses, about 2-3 oz each. See photo at right.

1 box vanilla or banana pudding mix. Cooked pudding works best.
2 cups cold milk
2 cups fresh strawberries
2/3 cup sugar
2 tbsp cornstarch
2/3 cup water
several drops red food coloring

To make the strawberry glaze:
In a food processor, blender or with an electric mixer, blend one cup chopped strawberries and 2/3 cup water until smooth. Add additional water to make mixture of 1-1/2 cups.

In a medium saucepan, combine sugar and cornstarch; blend in berry mixture. Cook and stir until thick and bubbly; cook another 2 minutes. Add several drops of red food coloring. Cool several minutes.

You can substitute the cooked strawberry glaze from above with a package of store bought strawberry glaze.

Make the pudding as directed on the package. Fill each dessert dish about half full with pudding, then layer with several slices of strawberries. Top with the strawberry glaze until covered. Refrigerate a couple of hours. Garnish with a dollop of whipped topping and a fresh strawberry. Serve and Enjoy!

Black Forest Cream Parfaits

For those of you who love the combined taste of chocolate and raspberries, this one is for you. Creamy smooth and so yummy. You will need 12 parfait shooter glasses, about 2-3 oz each. See photo at right.

1 cup raspberry preserves or jam
4 oz semi-sweetened chocolate pieces
3 tbsp milk
1 package (8 oz) cream cheese, softened
1 - 8 oz container whipped topping, leave out a couple of spoonfuls for garnish

In a microwavable bowl, add milk or water and chocolate pieces, heat until melted. Stir occasionally, careful not to burn. Add cream cheese and blend thoroughly. Gently fold in all but the few spoonfuls of the whipped topping until smooth and well blended.

I like using the Dessert Pro, mentioned earlier in the preparation section, it makes it so easy to layer. A wide mouth funnel will also work.

Either way, carefully spoon chocolate mixture into parfaits, layering chocolate mixture and then a teaspoon of raspberry jam, more chocolate and finishing with a layer of jam. Refrigerate until chilled. Garnish with a dollop of whipped topping and then a little drizzle of raspberry jam on top or just finish off with a fresh raspberry. Serve and Enjoy !

Chocolate Peanut Butter Parfait

This is another great recipe for those that love the peanut butter chocolate taste. Very light and creamy. You will need 12 parfait shooter glasses, about 2-3 oz. See photo at right.

1-1/2 cups finely crushed chocolate wafers or chocolate graham crackers
4 tbsp butter, melted
1 tbsp honey
1 pkg 8 oz cream cheese, softened
1/2 cup peanut butter
1 cup powdered sugar
3 tbsp milk
1 tsp vanilla
1 container 8 oz whipped topping or fresh made whipping cream
1/2 cup chocolate chips or 1/2 cup chocolate ice cream syrup
1/4 cup finely chopped peanuts

Combine melted butter, honey and crushed wafers in a mixing bowl. Fill each shooter glass with a heaping teaspoon of wafer mixture, about a 1/2" and pack down slightly.

Add a few chocolate chips or drizzle with chocolate syrup. Add some chopped peanuts on top of the cookie crumbs.

Combine cream cheese and peanut butter until smooth. Add powdered sugar, milk and vanilla. Mix together until well blended. You may need to add a little more milk to make this creamy. Gently fold in whipped topping or whipped cream.

Carefully spoon cheese mixture into the shooter glasses or use the Dessert Pro from page 16. Garnish with chocolate shavings or add another drizzle of chocolate syrup and some chopped peanuts. Refrigerate a couple of hours until set. Serve and Enjoy !

Snappy Fruit Yogurt Parfaits

This is another one of my favorites. It's really delicious in the morning or for brunch and is very easy to prepare. You will need 12 of the mini parfait glasses, about 2-3 oz each. See photo at right.

16 oz plain or vanilla yogurt
8 oz granola
48 blueberries and/or one cup of sliced strawberries or raspberries.

You can use almost any fresh fruit that can be cut into small pieces to fit into the parfait shooter glass. Try pineapple, cantaloupe, raspberries, peaches, pears, raisins, etc.

Add about a 1/4" of granola to each shooter glass, then add a 1/2" layer of yogurt and finally about 3 blueberries or strawberry slices or both. Add another layer of granola, yogurt and berries.

The crunchy granola will soften after awhile. If you do not like this, layer the yogurt and fresh fruit and put all the granola on top.

Refrigerate. Serve and Enjoy !

Cheesecakes, Custards & Mousse

Fluffy 2-Step Cherry Cheesecake

This is definitely one of my favorites. It is a very easy and simple no bake cherry cheese-cake dessert. I chose to make it in the mini flare footed dessert dishes, but any small glass container will work just fine. You will need 12 of these dessert dishes, about 2-3 oz each. See photo at right.

1 - 8 oz pkg cream cheese, softened or as an alternative, use ricotta cheese
1/3 cup sugar
1 tsp vanilla or almond extract
8 oz whipped topping
1 can cherry pie filling or any fruit pie filling

1 cup graham cracker crumbs, 3 tbsp butter, 1 tsp sugar

Melt butter in a microwaveable bowl, add sugar and cracker crumbs, mix thoroughly. Place a heaping teaspoon of cracker mixture in the bottom of dessert dish and pat down.

Mix cream cheese, vanilla and sugar in large bowl with wire whisk or electric mixer until smooth. Gently fold in whipped topping. Spoon in dessert dishes to almost full, just below the top. Add cherry filling to top it off. Serve and Enjoy !

Lemon Cloud

This is a very creamy and lemony flavored dessert. I love using the little cordial glasses to serve this dessert. It really adds a little flair to the presentation. You will need 12 of these small dessert dishes, about 4 oz each. See photo at right. This can be made with or without the graham cracker crust bottom.

3/4 cup sugar	3 tbsp cornstarch
1 cup water	1/4 cup lemon juice
2 egg yolks, slightly beaten	4 oz cream cheese, softened
1 tbsp grated lemon peel	1 cup whipped topping

1 cup graham cracker crumbs, 3 tbsp butter, 1 tsp sugar for crust.

Melt butter in a microwaveable bowl; add sugar and cracker crumbs; mix thoroughly.

In a medium saucepan, combine 3/4 cup sugar and cornstarch, mix well. Stir in water, lemon juice and egg yolks. Cook over medium heat until mixture boils and thickens, stirring constantly. Boil one more minute. Add cream cheese and lemon peel, stirring until cream cheese is melted and smooth. Cool slightly.

Add 1/2 cup whipped topping into the lemon mixture, mix well.

Place a heaping teaspoon of crumbs in bottom of the glass, press down with the end of a wooden spoon. Fill dessert dish with lemon mixture. Refrigerate for a few hours. When serving, top with a dollop of whipped topping or powdered sugar. Serve and Enjoy !

Quick & Simple Mousse

This is one of my favorite mini desserts. I make it all the time when I'm having friends over. I sometimes make 2 or 3 different flavors. It's very easy and really delicious. This can be made with almost any fruit flavoring; strawberry, raspberry, peach, pineapple, orange, lemon or key lime. You will need 12 shot glasses (2-3 oz each) or small glass cordials. See photo at right.

1 cup graham cracker crumbs, 3 tbsp butter and 1 tbsp sugar

1 package (8 oz) cream cheese, softened
1 container (8 oz) whipped topping
1/4 tsp vanilla
1 cup fresh or frozen fruit or 3 tbsp of grated citrus rind

Melt butter in a microwaveable bowl, add cracker crumbs and sugar, mix thoroughly. Place about a heaping teaspoon of mixture in the bottom of each shot glass; a little more for cordials. Press down.

In a large mixing bowl, beat softened cream cheese and vanilla until fluffy. Gently fold in whipped topping.

Now here is where you get creative ! Decide what flavor of mousse you want. You can also divide this recipe in half and make 2 different flavors.

For a fruit flavor, add about one cup of chopped fresh or frozen fruit to the cream mixture and gently fold in, if you want it creamier, mix it longer.

For citrus flavor, add a few tablespoons of finely grated rind and 1 tablespoon juice to the cream cheese mixture. Mix well.

Fill each shot glass to the top with your flavored mousse. Garnish with a dollop of whipped topping, if desired. Finish with a piece of fresh fruit, small cookie, etc. Serve and Enjoy !

Quick & Simple Chocolate Mousse

This is another very easy and just as delicious, chocolate dessert. Rich and very creamy. You can make it with dark, semi-sweet or sweet chocolate, depending on the intensity of your desired chocolate flavor. I usually use semi-sweet chocolate, the mousse is sweet, but not too sweet. You will need 12 shot glasses (2 oz each) or small glass cordials. See photo at right.

1 cup graham cracker crumbs, 3 tbsp butter and 1 tbsp sugar

1 package (8 oz) cream cheese, softened
1 container (8 oz) whipped topping
1/4 tsp vanilla
4 oz baking chocolate or chocolate chips
1 tbsp milk or water for melting chocolate

Melt butter in a microwaveable bowl, add cracker crumbs and sugar, mix thoroughly. Place about a teaspoon of mixture in the bottom of each shot glass, a little more for cordials. Press down.

In a large mixing bowl, beat softened cream cheese and vanilla until fluffy.

In another smaller microwaveable mixing bowl, melt together milk and chocolate until melted and creamy.

Add chocolate to cream cheese mixture, mix thoroughly. Gently fold in whipped topping.

Fill each shot glass to the top with the chocolate mousse. I use my Dessert Pro filling tool with the star tip and it will create a wonderful swirl effect with the mousse. You can garnish with a dollop of whipped topping, if desired. Finish off with a few shavings of chocolate or a chocolate wafer. Serve and Enjoy !

Raspberry Almond Cheesecake

This is another one of those quick and easy no bake cheesecake type desserts that look and taste absolutely delicious. I use fresh raspberries, but you can use almost any fresh fruit, try strawberries, blueberries, fresh pineapple or peaches. I love to make them in the little shot glasses, they're just bite size, well, maybe 2 or 3 bites. You will need 12 small shot glasses, about 2-3 oz each. See photo at right.

1 cup graham cracker crumbs, 3 tbsp butter, 1 tsp. sugar

8 oz cream cheese	8 oz ready to serve vanilla frosting
1 tbsp lemon juice	1 tbsp grated lemon peel
36-48 raspberries	1-1/2 cups whipped topping
handful of sliced or chopped almonds	

You can also use any prepared raspberry pie filling or preserves for topping.

Melt butter in a microwaveable bowl, add sugar and cracker crumbs, mix thoroughly. Place about a heaping spoonful of mixture in the bottom of the shot glass and pat down.

Mix softened cream cheese, vanilla frosting, lemon juice and lemon peel in a large mixing bowl at medium speed with an electric mixer. Fold in whipped topping until blended. Fill each shot glass with cream cheese mixture almost to the top. Chill until firm. Put 3-4 raspberries on top and some almond slices around the rim for garnish. Serve and Enjoy !

White Chocolate Devil's Food Dessert

This is another chocolate lover's dream: smooth and creamy, using both white and dark chocolate layered over chocolate graham cracker crust. I use the wonderful little mini glass bowls to really show off the layering effect. You will need 12 of these mini-dessert bowls, about 4 oz each. See photo on next page.

2 cups graham cracker crumbs, 4 tbsp butter, 1 tsp cocoa, 4 tbsp sugar

4 cups cold milk, divided in 2 cup portions
1 large pkg dark chocolate instant or cooked pudding
1 large pkg white chocolate instant or cooked pudding
1 - 8 oz container whipped topping, divided in half
1/4 cup chopped up chocolate chips or baking chocolate for garnish

You can use vanilla pudding if you cannot find white chocolate pudding.

Mix cracker crumbs, melted butter, cocoa and sugar in a mixing bowl. Divide the cracker mixture equally between the 12 dishes. Press down firmly in bottom of each dish.

Prepare the white chocolate pudding as directed on the box. The mixture will thicken quickly. Gently stir in half the whipped topping. Divide this mixture equally into the 12 dishes on top of the cracker layer. Refrigerate immediately so it will quick set.

Prepare the dark chocolate pudding the same as the white chocolate pudding from above but without adding the whipped topping. Pour the dark chocolate pudding over the white chocolate pudding. Refrigerate until set.

Garnish with a dollop of whipped topping and/or chocolate shavings. Serve and Enjoy !

Classic Cheesecake

The beauty of this simple cheesecake recipe is that you can leave it plain or top it with fresh fruit as I have pictured to the right. You will need 12 small 3 oz ramekins, suitable for baking. See photo at right.

Preheat oven to 350 degrees

For a simple graham cracker crust, you will need:
1 cup graham cracker crumbs, 1/4 cup margarine melted, 1/4 cup sugar

1 - 8 oz package cream cheese, softened or you can use ricotta cheese
3/4 cup sour cream
2 tsp vanilla
2 egg whites
3/4 cup white sugar
1 can of cherry or blueberry pie filling or use fresh berries for topping (optional)

Mix the crust ingredients together and divide the mixture equally between the 12 ramekins and press down.

Beat cream cheese, sugar and vanilla in large mixing bowl with electric mixer until well blended. Add egg whites, mix well. Then add sour cream and mix thoroughly. Pour equally into the 12 ramekins, almost to the top.

Bake 20 minutes or until center is almost set. Turn off oven, leaving oven door open for another 15 minutes. Remove from oven and refrigerate until chilled. When ready to serve, top each ramekin with a spoonful of pie filling or fresh berries. Serve and Enjoy !

Lemon Chiffon Dessert

If you like the taste of lemon and who doesn't, you will love this dessert. Velvety smooth and not real sweet. The orange version is equally as delicious. You will need 12 mini dessert dishes, about 2-3 oz each. I chose the little shot glasses; they are small and so cute. They serve just enough of this tangy dessert to compliment your other specialties. See photo at right.

3 egg yolks, slightly beaten
1 cup water
1/4 cup sugar
1 pkg (3 oz) lemon gelatin
2 tbsp lemon juice
1/2 cup water

3 egg whites
dash of salt
1/4 cup sugar

4 tsp grated lemon rind, divide in half

Combine egg yolks and one cup water in saucepan, add 1/4 cup sugar. Cook and stir over low heat until mixture slightly thickens and just comes to a boil. Remove from heat. Add gelatin and stir until dissolved. Add 1/2 cup water, lemon juice and 2 tsp lemon rind. Stir thoroughly and chill until slightly thickened.

In another mixing bowl, beat egg whites and salt until foamy. Gradually beat in 1/4 cup sugar and continue beating until mixture stands at peaks. Combine the 2 mixtures together. Blend well. Spoon into dessert dishes and chill until firm, about 2-3 hours. Garnish with the remaining grated lemon rind or a dollop of whipped topping. Serve and Enjoy !

Orange Chiffon Dessert

Substitute orange gelatin, orange juce and orange rind and follow directions from above.

Simple Creme Brulee

Creme Brulee is another classic dessert, so when you serve it in the mini ceramic ramekins, it makes it even more special. You will need 12 of the 3 oz ramekins to make this recipe. Make sure the ramekins are suitable for baking. See photo at right.

preheat oven to 325 degrees

warm together:
1 cup heavy cream
1 cup half and half
2 tbsp sugar
1 tsp vanilla

whisk together:
3 egg yolks
1 egg
1/4 cup sugar
pinch of salt

Some cinnamon sugar or nutmeg is needed for topping or about a cup of fresh sliced strawberries or raspberries, both are optional.

Warm cream, half & half, sugar and vanilla in a saucepan over medium heat just until steam rises. Do not boil.

In a mixing bowl, whisk together the yolks, one egg, 1/4 cup of the sugar and pinch of salt.

Combine both mixtures and divide among the 12 ramekins. Arrange the ramekins in a large baking dish filled with a 1/4" of hot water. Carefully transfer the baking dish to the oven. Bake custards 20-30 minutes or until just set. The centers will jiggle slightly with a touch of the finger. Do not overcook.

Remove ramekins from dish and let cool. Wrap with plastic wrap. Chill until completely cold or overnight. Remove any moisture with paper towel and sprinkle with cinnamon sugar or nutmeg before serving or you can add some fresh raspberries or strawberries to the top. Serve and Enjoy !

Simple Lemon Ginger Creme Brulee

This is a wonderful variation of the classic creme brulee from the previous page, just by adding a slight tangy lemon twist to the flavor. It's so wonderful and very creamy. This recipe makes 12 servings in the 3 oz ramekins. Again, make sure they are suitable for baking. See photo at right.

preheat oven to 325 degrees

warm together:
1 cup heavy cream
1 cup half and half
2 tbsp sugar
1/4 tsp ground ginger
1/4 cup lemon rind finely grated

whisk together:
3 egg yolks
1 egg
1/4 cup sugar
1/4 tsp ginger & a pinch of salt

Warm together cream, half & half, sugar, lemon rind and ginger in a saucepan over medium heat just until steam rises, do not boil. Let stand for 15 minutes.

In a mixing bowl, whisk together the yolks, one egg, sugar, ginger and salt.

Combine both mixtures, mixing thoroughly. Divide among the 12 ramekins. Arrange the ramekins so they do not touch, in a large baking dish with 2" sides filled with a 1/4" of hot water. Carefully transfer the baking dish to the oven. Bake custards at 325 degrees for 20-30 minutes or until just set. The centers will jiggle slightly with a touch of the finger. Do not overcook.

Remove ramekins from dish and let cool. Wrap with plastic wrap. Chill until completely cold or overnight. Remove any moisture with paper towel and sprinkle with powdered sugar and lemon rind twist. Serve and Enjoy !

Lemony Cheesecake

Some delicious little lemon cheesecakes with a wonderful lemony flavored glaze. It's a little more time consuming, but really worth every minute of it. The recipe makes 12 individual 2-3 oz ramekins, make sure the ramekins are suitable for baking. See photo at right.

Preheat oven to 350 degrees

Cheesecake:
non-stick vegetable oil spray
3/4 cup sugar
1/4 cup lemon juice
4 tsp finely grated lemon peel
1 8 oz pkg cream cheese, softened
1/2 cup whole milk
1 egg
3/4 cup sour cream
1 cup lemon curd or vanilla yogurt or whipping cream for topping

Lemon Curd or Glaze:
2 beaten eggs
1/2 cup sugar
2 tsp cornstarch
2 tsp finely grated lemon rind
1/4 cup butter or margarine
1/4 cup lemon juice

Spray ramekins with nonstick spray. Using an electric mixer, beat sugar and lemon juice until sugar dissolves. Add milk, cream cheese and sour cream, beat until smooth. Beat in egg and lemon rind until well blended.

Divide batter among the 12 ramekins, place on rimmed cookie sheet. Bake until puffed and set in center, about 18-20 minutes. Chill until cold, about 2 hours.

To make Lemon Curd: In a saucepan, combine sugar and cornstarch, stir in lemon juice and lemon rind. Add margarine. Cook until thick and bubbly. Add the beaten egg a little at a time. Stir and cook for 2 minutes. Cover and cool.

Spread lemon curd over each ramekin or use yogurt or whipped topping.

Serve and Enjoy !

Chocolate French Silk Delight

This is a rich and creamy chocolate dessert that will please anyone in love with chocolate. I love to serve it in the footed flare dish because is makes it look so special and appetizing. You will need 12 of these mini dessert dishes, 3 oz each. See photo at right.

4 oz semi-chocolate, cut into pieces
1 tbsp milk or water
1 cup butter, not margarine, softened
3/4 cup sugar
1 tsp vanilla
1-1/2 cup egg substitute
1/4 cup cream

1/2 cup whipped topping for garnish
1 oz chocolate, shaved

Melt chocolate in a microwaveable bowl with 1 tbsp milk or water.

In another larger mixing bowl, melt butter and gradually add sugar. Beat until light and fluffy with an electric mixer. Add melted chocolate, cream and vanilla, mix well. Add egg product half at a time to mixture. With electric mixer, whip until smooth and fluffy.

Spoon into the small dessert dishes. Refrigerate. Finish off with whipped topping and chocolate pieces when ready to serve. Enjoy !

Fruit Desserts

Honey Fruit Compote

This is a delicious dessert but it is also a very refreshing salad. Serve it in these mini glass bowls, it shows off all the cool colors. The recipe fills at least 12 small glass bowls, 4 oz each. See photo at right.

2 cups diced fresh pineapple or canned pineapple tidbits
1 cup diced honeydew and or cantaloupe melon
1 cup diced mango
2 tbsp chopped fresh basil
2 tbsp lime juice
4 tbsp honey
1 tbsp chopped fresh mint
1/4 cup finely chopped red bell pepper
1/4 tsp ginger
1 tbsp sesame seeds, optional

Mix the lime juice, ginger and honey together. Then mix all ingredients except sesame seeds in a large mixing bowl. Toss the fruit with the honey and juice mixture. Let stand 10-15 minutes. Divide mixture among the 12 small glass dishes as shown on next page. Sprinkle with sesame seeds. Serve and Enjoy !

Peaches & Cream

This is a very light and refreshing little mini dessert. You can use almost any fruit and complimenting gelatin. You will need 12 small glass dessert dishes, about 2-3 oz each. I love the little shot glasses for this recipe. See photo at right.

1 cup graham cracker crumbs
2 tbsp butter or margarine
1/4 cup sugar

1 package of cream cheese, softened
1 - 3 oz pkg peach flavored gelatin
1 cup chopped peaches (15 oz can) or crushed pineapple, drained thoroughly
1 - 8 oz container of whipped topping, you will need 6 oz for recipe

Combine cracker crumbs, 1/4 cup sugar and melted butter, mix together. Spoon about a heaping teaspoon into the bottom of the shot glasses, flatten down slightly.

Mix cream cheese and dry gelatin with an electric mixer until well blended. Add chopped peaches and 6 oz whipped topping, mix thoroughly. Save a few peach pieces for garnish.

Spoon into the glass dishes as pictured at right and garnish with a piece of peach. Refrigerate a few hours or until firm. Keep leftovers refrigerated. Serve and Enjoy !

Pineapple & Cream

Use fresh, crushed or canned pineapple chunks, drained thoroughly. Use pineapple gelatin instead of peach gelatin. Otherwise, follow recipe from above. Serve and Enjoy !

Berry Cream Parfait

This is a small simple little dessert that can be made quickly and served immediately but it is also just as delicious if you make it a few hours ahead of time. I've even made it the day before and refrigerated it. I love to serve it in little shot glasses. They are just the perfect size. You will need 12 of these small shot glasses. See photo at right.

1 cup graham cracker crumbs, 3 tbsp butter, 1 tsp sugar

1 can cherry, peach or blueberry pie filling
1 - 8 oz pkg cream cheese, softened
1 pkg vanilla instant pie filling
1 cup cold milk
8 oz whipped topping, divided in two

Mix cracker crumbs, melted butter and sugar in a mixing bowl. Divide the cracker mixture equally between the 12 shot glasses; press down firmly in bottom of each dish.

Spread a tablespoon of pie filling in bottom of each dish.

Mix softened cream cheese and milk in large mixing bowl. Stir in pudding and mix thoroughly. Gently stir in half of the whipped topping.

Fill each dessert dish with the cream cheese mixture and top off with the remaining pie filling. Refrigerate 2 hours or until set. Add a dollop of whipped topping to each before serving. Serve and Enjoy !

Banana Caramel Delight

This is a wonderful old family recipe I borrowed from the Traxler Family of Carey, Ohio. It is pretty simple but is bursting with flavor. If you can serve this dessert immediately, add a small scoop of vanilla ice cream before the other ingredients. It will blow you away. The original recipe is listed below. You will need 12 small glass dessert bowls, 4 oz each. See photo at right.

4-6 ripe bananas (firm) sliced
1/2 cup dark brown sugar
2 egg whites
2 tsp vinegar
3 tbsp water
1/2 cup chopped pecans or peanuts

Mix together in a microwaveable bowl or small sauce pan the brown sugar, egg whites, vinegar and water. Cook until hot, stirring a few times. Do not let boil. Let cool slightly.

For a quick version of this, but not quite as tasty, use a caramel sauce instead of the mixture from above.

Place 5-6 slices of bananas in each dish; drizzle cooled sugar mixture or caramel sauce over bananas and sprinkle with nut pieces. It's that simple. Serve and Enjoy !

Quick & Easy Desserts

Chocolate Praline Fantasy

This is one of those desserts that is so rich and delicious you won't be able to make them fast enough. A delicious combination of caramel, chocolate and pecans. It doesn't get any better than this. I love to use the footed flare dish, it makes a fabulous presentation. You will need 12 small glass dessert dishes, 2-3 oz each. See photo at right.

1 cup chocolate wafer crumbs
1/4 cup butter or margarine
2 tbsp sugar
30 caramels
1/2 cup caramel ice cream topping
1/4 cup whipping cream or heavy cream
2 cups coarsely chopped pecans or use the halves
3/4 cup semi-sweet chocolate pieces
1/4 cup whipping cream or heavy cream
1/4 tsp milk

Melt butter in a microwaveable bowl, then add chocolate cracker crumbs and sugar, mix thoroughly. Place a good tablespoon of mixture in the bottom of dessert dish and press down.

In a heavy saucepan, melt caramels in the caramel ice cream topping over low heat until melted. Stir in 1/4 cup of whipping cream. Remove from heat and add the chopped pecans. Spoon into dessert dishes to about half full while it is still warm.

For the topping, in a small heavy saucepan or microwaveable bowl, melt chocolate and milk slowly, stir in the other 1/4 cup whipping cream. Drizzle chocolate sauce over the pecan mixture in a criss-cross pattern. Serve and Enjoy !

Coconut Cream Delight

This is a coconut lover's dream: a smooth and creamy coconut filling on top of a crunchy bed of homemade granola. I love this dessert served in the mini parfaits. You will need 12 of these mini parfaits dishes, 2-3 oz each. See photo at right.

8 oz cream cheese, softened
1 tbsp sugar
1/4 cup milk
1 cup flaked coconut (save 1/4 cup to toast for garnish)
8 oz whipped topping
1/2 tsp almond or vanilla extract

1 cup oatmeal, uncooked
3 tbsp butter
1 tbsp dark brown sugar
2 tbsp flour
1/4 cup finely chopped peanuts, almonds or pecans

In a mixing bowl, add butter, sugar, oatmeal, flour and nuts, mix thoroughly until crumbly. Place about a heaping teaspoon of crumbs in bottom of each dessert dish, press down with the end of a wooden spoon.

Mix together cream cheese, vanilla and sugar, gradually mix in milk. Beat until smooth. Fold in 3/4 cup coconut and then the whipped topping.

To toast the coconut, spread about a 1/4 cup on a cookie sheet and put in oven broiler for a few minutes until slightly browned.

Fill shot glass with coconut mixture and add toasted coconut on top for garnish. Refrigerate one hour. Serve and Enjoy !

Banana Cream Delight

This is a quick and simple dessert that will remind you of a delicious banana cream pie, only it is served in a mini dessert dish. You will need 12 mini-dessert dishes 2-3 oz each. See photo at right.

1 cup graham cracker crumbs, 3 tbsp butter, 2 tbsp sugar
1 large box vanilla or banana pudding, cooked type is creamier
2 cups milk
5-6 bananas, sliced
1 container whipped topping

Mix cracker crumbs, melted butter and sugar in a mixing bowl. Divide the cracker mixture equally between the 12 dishes, press down firmly in bottom of each dish.

Put 5-6 slices of banana in the bottom of each dessert dish. Make the pudding as directed on the box, it will start to set up rather quickly. Cover bananas with pudding, chill until set, about an hour. Cover pudding with whipped topping. Serve and Enjoy !

Fluffy Fruit Dessert

This recipe has been served at every family get together for as long as I can remember. It is called by a variety of different names. No matter what you call it or how you make it, it's always a light and delicious dessert. It looks great served in these mini flare dishes. You will need 12 of these 2-3 oz dessert dishes. See photo at right.

1 can pineapple chunks or tid-bits, drained
1 can mandarin oranges, drained
1 can sliced peaches, cubed and drained
1 cup miniature marshmallows
1/4 cup maraschino cherries, cut in half
1 cup whipped topping or vanilla yogurt

For a different twist, try adding sliced seedless grapes, shredded coconut, diced apples or some chopped pecans.

In a large mixing bowl, add all the different fruits and marshmallows. Make sure the fruits are all drained thoroughly. Sometimes I lay the fruit pieces on a few layers of paper towel and let them drain. Gently fold in the whipped topping or yogurt. Fill each of the mini footed bowls and garnish with an additional maraschino cherry. Serve and Enjoy !

.

Tropical Pineapple Orange Delight

I have always served this light and fluffy dessert during the summer because it is so refreshing, but it is really great anytime. It looks especially festive served in the footed mini dish. You will need 12 small dessert dishes, 3-4 oz each. See photo at right.

1 - 20 oz can of crushed pineapple with juice
1 box (3 oz) package vanilla instant pudding
1 can mandarin oranges, drained
1 container (8 oz) whipped topping
12 maraschino cherries for garnish
1 pound cake or angel food cake

Cut the cake into small 1" square pieces. Place a small square of cake in the bottom of the dessert dish.

Cut up the mandarin oranges into small bite size pieces. Mix the orange pieces, pineapple, pineapple juice and instant pudding together. Gently fold in the whipped topping. Spoon into small dessert dishes over the cake. Garnish with a maraschino cherry on top. Can be served immediately or refrigerate for an hour or so. Serve and Enjoy !

Cranberry Mellow Delight

This dessert combines the sweet taste of marshmallows and the tangy taste of cranberries, combined together to make a delicious dessert or salad. I like to serve it in mini glass bowls to show off the colors and the texture of the cranberry mixture. You will need 12 small glass bowls, 3-4 oz each. See photo at right.

6 oz pkg raspberry gelatin	2 cups boiling water, 1 cup cold water
16 oz can whole cranberry sauce	1/2 cup milk
4 cups miniature marshmallows	1 tsp vanilla
16 oz can of crushed pineapple, drained	4 oz whipped topping
few drops of green food coloring	

Dissolve gelatin in 2 cups boiling water, stir for about 2 minutes. Stir in 1 cup cold water or a cup of ice cubes. Refrigerate 1 hour or so until thickened. Stir in cranberry sauce and crushed pineapple (drained). Pour mixture into the dessert dishes about 2/3 full. Refrigerate 3 hours until set.

Microwave marshmallows and milk in a microwaveable bowl for 3-4 minutes until melted and smooth, stirring every minute or so. Stir in vanilla and green food coloring. Gently fold in the whipped topping until smooth. Fill dessert dishes to the top with marshmallow mixture. Refrigerate one hour and serve.

For a added twist, try adding chopped celery, apples, oranges or pecans.

You can also substitute a jar of marshmallow creme for the miniature marshmallows, just omit the milk. Add the whipped topping to 2 cups marshmallow cream. Continue recipe. Garnish if desired. Serve and Enjoy !

Cherry Chiffon Dessert

This is a great mini dessert for a large family gathering. It makes a rather large portion so you can fill anywhere from 12 to 20 small shot glasses, 2-3 oz each. See photo to right.

You can also use strawberry or peach pie filling instead of cherry.

Using sweetened condensed milk will make the dessert very rich tasting; use vanilla yogurt to make it less rich. This dessert is very tasty with or without the marshmallows.

1 - 21 oz can of cherry pie filing
1 can sweetened condensed milk or 12 oz plain or vanilla yogurt
8 oz whipped topping
1 - 20 oz can crushed pineapple, drained
1 cup miniature marshmallows, optional
some maraschino cherries for garnish, optional

Combine the crushed pineapple, condensed milk and marshmallows in a large mixing bowl until well blended. Add the whipped topping and mix together. Gently fold in the cherry pie filling. Spoon into the glass dessert dishes and chill. Garnish with a maraschino cherry if desired. Serve and Enjoy !

Simple Berry Shortcake

This is a simple yet traditional family favorite. Serving it in little mini bowls just makes it more festive. I'll sometimes make a few strawberry shortcakes and a few peach shortcakes. Maybe even throw in a few blueberries for color. They are simple and delicious. This recipe makes 12 servings in the small mini glass bowls, 4 oz each. See photo at right.

2 cups fresh berries (sliced strawberries, raspberries, blueberries, peaches) or any combination of each.

1 angel food cake, sponge cake, pound cake, biscuits or chocolate brownies

1 cup whipped topping

Cut up the cake into small bite size pieces or slices and put into the glass dishes. Spoon berries with juice over the cake. The more juice the better. Top with a dollop of whipping cream. Serve and Enjoy !

Cakes & Tarts

Quick & Easy Fruit Tart

This is one of my favorite mini desserts for the fall season: little fruit tarts that will please everyone. I'll make a variety of them for a get together, a few apple, cherry and peach. Make a bunch, they will go quickly. You will need 12 small ceramic ramekins, 2-3 oz each. Make sure the ramekins are suitable for baking. See photo at right. Preheat oven to 350 degrees.

Use any kind of fresh fruit (strawberries, raspberries, blueberries, apples or peaches). You can also use canned fruit or pie filling.

3 cups of cleaned sliced fruit (do not slice the raspberries or blueberries)

1/4 cup flour	1/2 cup flour
1/2 cup sugar	1/4 cup sugar
1/4 tsp almond extract	1/4 cup brown sugar
pinch of cinnamon for the apples or peach tarts	3 tbsp butter or margarine

In a large mixing bowl, combine 1/4 cup flour, sugar and cinnamon (if needed). Add sliced fruit and almond extract, toss gently until well coated. Place enough fruit into the ramekin to almost full.

If you use canned pie filling, omit the flour, sugar and almond extract that is mixed with the fruit. I still add a little cinnamon even to canned pie filling.

Crumb Topping
In another mixing bowl, combine 1/2 cup flour and both sugars. Cut in or crumble butter with a pastry blender or a fork until it is crumbly. Cover the top of each ramekin with crumb mixture. Place ramekins on a cookie sheet. Bake in the oven at 350 degrees until just bubbly, about 20 minutes. Do not overbake, crunchy fruit is better than soggy fruit. Sometimes I just sprinkle the top with plain granola instead of making the crumb topping. You will need about a cup of granola to cover 12 ramekins. Let cool. Serve and Enjoy !

Chocolate Raspberry Tart

This is another one of those delicious chocolate and raspberry desserts that is very choco-latey and rich, but smooth as silk. This recipe makes 12 servings in small glass dessert dishes, 2-3 oz each. See photo at right.

9 whole chocolate graham crackers or plain chocolate shortbread cookies,
          (about a cup of coarse crumbs)
3 tbsp butter or margarine, melted
2-3 tbsp honey

2 cups (16 oz) whipping cream
12 oz semi-sweet chocolate chips
2 tbsp unsweetened cocoa powder
1/4 cup sugar
1 cup fresh raspberries or 1/2 cup raspberry jam

Crush graham crackers and mix with 3 tbsp butter and honey. Sometimes I just mix with lots of honey, without using butter. Divide equally in the bottom of the 12 small dishes, pack firmly down.

In a heavy saucpan, bring the whipping cream just to a boil, reduce heat to low and sim-mer 5 minutes, stirring constantly. Add chocolate chips, sugar and cocoa powder and mix until smooth and melted. Pour chocolate mixture into each dish over crust. Chill 1-2 hours or until firm.

Can be served with fresh raspberries, raspberry puree or raspberry preserves on top. Serve and Enjoy !

Chocolate Fantasy

I borrowed this wonderful recipe from a former associate of mine, Carol Karmel. She also makes the best chocolate chip cookies. All I did to her recipe was adapt it to these little mini bowls. It's delicious and very easy to make. You will need 12 small glass bowls, 4 oz each. See photo at right.

Purchase a devil's food chocolate cake or bake a chocolate cake from any cake mix in a 9x13 pan. You will not use all the 9x13 cake.

1 can sweetened condensed milk
1 jar of caramel sundae sauce
1 bag of toffee chips or pieces
1/4 cup pecans, finely chopped, optional
1 - 8 oz container of whipped topping
maraschino cherries for garnish

In a mixing bowl, mix together the sweetened condensed milk with the caramel sauce, set aside.

Cut the cake into 2" squares, about 1" thick, just large enough to fit into the bottom of the small glass dish.

Poke four holes with the handle of a wood spoon into the piece of cake. Pour about two tablespoons of the caramel sauce over the cake, letting it go down over the sides and into the holes. Sprinkle some of the toffee chips on top and some pecan pieces. Follow this with a generous helping of whipped topping and then a few more of the toffee pieces and a cherry for garnish. Serve and Enjoy !

Summer Fruit Cake

This is a very light and refreshing summer dessert, very tasty when fresh strawberries are at the height of the season. You will need 12 small dessert bowls, 4 oz each. They really show off the colorful dessert so well. See photo at right.

12 small 1" square pieces of yellow pound cake or angel food cake
15-20 fresh strawberries, sliced
4 bananas, sliced
10 oz can crushed pineapple, drained and save the juice
1/2 can of mandarin oranges, drained and cut into pieces
1/2 box of instant vanilla pudding (not the cooked type)
8 oz whipped topping, divided in half

In a large mixing bowl, mix together the pineapple, 1/2 the pineapple juice, oranges and vanilla pudding. Mix thoroughly. Add half the whipped topping, fold together. This will set up rather quickly.

Place the small square of cake in the bottom of the dessert dish. Drizzle with a little pineapple juice. Then top with a heaping spoonful of pudding and pineapple mixture. Add 3-4 slices of bananas and a few strawberry slices on top of the pudding mixture. Cover the strawberries and bananas with another layer of pudding mixture.

Leave 12 slices of strawberries for garnish.

Garnish with a dollop of the whipped topping and a strawberry slice on top. Refrigerate. Serve and Enjoy !

Tiramisu (Quick & Easy)

This will look a little different from the traditional Italian Tiramisu, but it will taste just the same. I've taken a few short cuts, but in the end, it's quick and easy and tastes just delicious. You will need 12 small glass dessert bowls, 4 oz each. See photo at right.

One pound cake (angel food cake or plain white cake will also work)

1/3 cup sugar
1/2 cup water
1 cup very strong black coffee
2 tbsp rum (optional)
1 tbsp coffee liqueur (optional)
1 container whipped topping
8 oz cream cheese, softened

1 tbsp honey
1 tsp vanilla
3 oz semi-sweet chocolate, melted
1 oz semi-sweet chocolate, shaved
1/2 cup powdered sugar
1/4 cup milk

Cut cake into 24 - 2" squares about a 1/2" thick

In a microwaveable measuring cup or mug, combine sugar, strong black coffee and honey. Heat slowly until it almost boils. Remove from heat and stir in rum, cool completely.

In a large mixing bowl, mix together softened cream cheese, powdered sugar, milk and vanilla. Stir in the 3 oz of the melted chocolate. Save the other 1 oz of chocolate to shave for garnish.

Place a piece of cake in each dessert dish. Drizzle about a tablespoon of coffee sauce over cake. Then a heaping spoon of cream cheese mixture on top of that and spread around. Then repeat these 2 steps again.

Mix whipped topping and coffee liqueur together and put a large spoon of this topping on top of the layers of cake. Sprinkle each with chocolate shavings. Can be served immediately or refrigerated. Serve and Enjoy !

Not Just For Kids !

Creamy Gelatin Parfaits

This is a really simple yet creamy and delicious gelatin dessert. What makes it extra special is serving it in a small cordial glass or mini parfait. You will need 12 cordials or parfait shooter glasses, 4 oz each. Something that will show the layers. See photo at right.

1 - 3 oz box any flavor red gelatin
1 - 3 oz box lemon or orange flavored gelatin
some fresh fruit: bananas, strawberries, peaches, etc., optional
1 - 8 oz container of whipped topping
3 cups boiling water
some ice cubes

In a mixing bowl, add 1 cup boiling water to one box of red gelatin, stir until dissolved, about 2 minutes. Add a 1/2 cup ice cubes. Stir until melted. Pour the gelatin into the cordial glasses until about half full. Refrigerate while making second box, this will help it set.

Add your favorite fresh or canned fruit if you want - it is just as festive plain.

Prepare the second box of gelatin as directed from above, except this time, instead of adding the ice cubes, add 1 cup of whipped topping. Mix thoroughly. Pour the mixture into each of the cordial glasses until full. Refrigerate about 2 hours or until set.

Top each with a dollop of remaining whipped topping. Serve and Enjoy !

Fruit Smoothie Delight

This is a very smooth and refreshing dessert that is great at breakfast or brunch. These also make great after school snacks for the kids. They can be made with almost any fruit. You will need 12 tall mini parfait shooter glasses, 2-3 oz each. See photo at right.

12 oz vanilla yogurt
6 oz whipped topping
12 oz bag frozen mixed berries, thawed
12 fresh raspberries or strawberries for garnish (optional)

Slightly chop or puree the mixed berries. Sometimes I put the fruit in a blender and then add the yogurt with a few ice cubes and the whipped topping. Puree until smooth.

Or you can just mix together yogurt and mixed berries and then fold in the whipped topping. Mix well.

Fill shooter glasses with yogurt mixture and add a berry on top for garnish. Refrigerate.

These are light and fluffy. Kids will love them, adults too. Serve and Enjoy !

Pudding Parfaits

I love making these little pudding parfaits. They are easy to make and a favorite with almost everyone. You can make them with almost any flavor pudding - be creative! You will need 12 parfait shooters or mini shot glasses, 2-3 oz each. See photo at right.

To get started you will need:

2 boxes of different flavored cooked pudding mix
       (cooked pudding is a little creamier than the instant type)
1 - 8 oz container of whipped topping
some chocolate chips, optional
chocolate shavings, for garnish

This recipe uses one box of chocolate and one vanilla. You can mix any 2 flavors you like. Try butterscotch and chocolate. The more contrast the better.

Mix the first box of pudding as directed on the package. Fill each shooter glass halfway full of pudding. Add some chocolate chips on top of pudding, optional.

Mix the second flavor of pudding as directed. Fill the parfaits to the top with the second flavor. Refrigerate for a couple of hours. Add a dollop of whipped topping and a few chocolate chips or shavings for garnish. Serve and Enjoy !

Comforting Gelatin Desserts

This is one of those old family favorites: Simple layered gelatin with your favorite fruit. Serving it in these little mini parfaits is just another way to make it extraordinary. You will need 12 unusual glass dessert dishes, shooters, cordials or shot glasses, 2-3 oz. See photo at right.

2 small boxes of gelatin, 2 different flavors - they will be made separately.

Any kind of fresh or canned fruit except pineapple
(the amount depends on the size of the dessert dish)

Some whipped topping for garnish

I like using 2 different flavors, like lime and orange. Make the lime gelatin as directed on the box. Fill the mini parfaits half full with the lime gelatin. Refrigerate until almost set.

Add your favorite fruit to the parfait glass. Try putting different fruit in each dessert dish.

Make the orange gelatin as directed on the box. I usually let it set for 30 minutes, until it slightly thickens before I pour the gelatin over the fruit. Refrigerate until set, about 2 hours. Add a dollop of whipped topping for garnish. Serve and Enjoy !

INDEX

About the author.

ROBERT ZOLLWEG is a native of Toledo, Ohio and has been entertaining professionally for many years. Writing this cookbook on Just Mini Desserts has been his dream and passion. A tabletop industry veteran for almost 40 years, he designs glassware, flatware and ceramic product for both the retail and foodservice industry. He has worked with all of the major retailers; Crate and Barrel, Pier One Imports, Williams-Sonoma, Macy's, Cost Plus World Market, Bed Bath & Beyond, JCPenneys, Target, Walmart and Sears to name a few. Most of his professional career has been spent with Libbey Glass in Toledo. Robert has traveled the world extensively looking for color and design trends and the right products to design and bring to the retail and foodservice marketplace. He is also an artist-painter in his spare time and works primarily with acrylic on canvass using bold colors. His painting style has been called by many as abstract expressionism. Robert's passion for entertaining extends into every aspect of his life, so Just Mini Desserts serves as the perfect continuation of that passion. He currently splits his time living in his historic home in Toledo's Historic Old West End and also in Saugatuck, Michigan.

Thank you for buying this book,

Enjoy !